# is it red?
# is it yellow?
# is it blue?

## an adventure in color by

# tana hoban

## greenwillow books

*An Imprint of* **HarperCollins** *Publishers*

Is it Red? Is it Yellow? Is it Blue?
Copyright © 1978 by Tana Hoban
Manufactured in China.
All rights reserved.
www.harperchildrens.com

Library of Congress
Cataloging in Publication Data
Hoban, Tana.
Is it red?
Is it yellow?
Is it blue?
"Greenwillow Books."
Summary: Illustrations and brief
text introduce colors and the
concepts of shape, quantity,
and direction.
ISBN 0-688-80171-4
ISBN 0-688-84171-6 (lib. bdg.)
ISBN 0-688-07034-5 (pbk.)
1. Colors—Juvenile literature.
2. Form perception—Juvenile
literature.   3. Space perception—
Juvenile literature.   (1. Colors.
2. Size and shape.   3. Space
perception.   4. Visual perception.)
I. Title.
BF311.H56   153.7'5   78-2549

25  24  23  22  21  20  19  18

to Jeffrey
and to David, Jeremy and Erica

**is it red? is it yellow? is it blue?**
an adventure in color

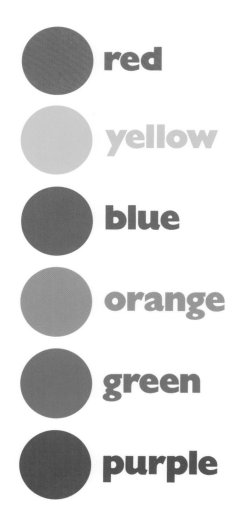

red

yellow

blue

orange

green

purple

Tana Hoban's photographs have been exhibited at the Museum of Modern Art. She has won many gold medals and prizes for her work as a photographer and filmmaker. And, of course, her books for children are known and loved throughout the world. These books include:

**SHAPES AND THINGS**

**LOOK AGAIN!**
1971 ALA Notable

**COUNT AND SEE**
1972 ALA Notable

**PUSH·PULL, EMPTY·FULL**

**OVER, UNDER & THROUGH**

**WHERE IS IT?**

**CIRCLES, TRIANGLES AND SQUARES**

**DIG·DRILL, DUMP·FILL**

**BIG ONES, LITTLE ONES**